MANY JUNIPERS, HEARTBEATS

Many Junipers, Heartbeats

Jane Miller

Copper Beech Press

Providence 1980

Of the poems in this volume, the "Nettles" sequence appeared in *Antaeus;* "A Winter of Love Letters and A Morning Prayer" in *The Agni Review.* Others appeared in the following publications, to which acknowledgement is here made: *The Antioch Review, Crazy Horse, Columbia, Intro 9, The Iowa Review, The Mississippi Review, The Nation, Ploughshares, Anthology of Magazine Verse and Yearbook of American Poetry for 1979, Woman Poet.*

ISBN: 0-914278-29-0

Copper Beech Press
Box 1852 Brown University
Providence, Rhode Island 02912

This book was made possible by a grant from the National Endowment for the Arts in Washington, D.C. (a federal agency).

Typeset by Ronna Johnson/Aspect Composition
13 Robinson St., Somerville, Mass. 02145

CONTENTS

Nettles

Saudade

A Winter of Love Letters and a Morning Prayer

Autumn, Exploded View

for Walter and Flossie

NETTLES

UNDER THE ZANZARIERE

She put the comb in one hand and with the left waved. With that
deliberate ambivalence I've come to hate. The slow kiss which lands
on my face like a wasp. It began in childhood. Mother desired her
and they spent hours together. If not in the garden surrounded by
dahlias and clover, inside the musty hallways or under the zanzariere.

They very deliberately excluded others, though I should say they
were kind to me. When they bathed I listened, not to their laughter
which in itself was omnivorous, but to the splashing, the pauses.
I had too much respect for Mother to be surprised. For example,
her choice of linden flowers for the bath.

They went on like this, conspicuous in the dark. They would brush
each other's long heavy hair. Mother was terribly young, but not
at all innocent, as you must realize. Once, on the terrace, a
liana plant straining toward light amused them. She let Claire
eat its flowers.

The thought of them upstairs in their horribly white chamber, with
late afternoon light, disgusted me. I began to study insects,
collecting their persistent voices, like whispers in another room.

BLACK MISTRESSES, WASPS

I pinned a horsefly under my shirt to quicken my heart—
no worse than *their* indiscretions. They crept out of Claire's room
into the stinking summer grass. During tea, always delayed because
Mother enjoyed Claire's impatience, they'd play with the honey.
Bees gathered like school girls, singing and jumping;

Mother would torture them by lowering the lid and clanging
a spoon on the lip. *To have to sit there, well-mannered.*
She wore a dark green dress with billows and curved entrances
in which Claire made a nest. I feigned nonchalance and lay
in a hammock. Mother read from *The Thousand and One Nights*

but it was an excruciating journey—exiles and witches in damask.
Claire flew out of Mother's pleats in a rage. I'd pull myself
tighter with invisible threads, burying a sound in my head until

it surrendered—my beloved, my stuffed hummingbird.

HOUSE WITH YELLOW SMOKE SONNET

Two daughters who seemed to be listening.
Was I the mother, was not this
our house? Nária half-slept
seeping out of a nightmare
like yellow smoke. Beyond that—

was it cold by the lake today?

the chill of this child
whose star dazzled elsewhere—
ash. I had to go without a single light.

May Claire's hair be down, may the lace canopy
never entirely cover her most perfect
quality, ennui.
                    Even as she sleeps
I trespass, counting the lonely mansion railings
of her spine.

LIES

Probably no one noticed the mornings I disappeared to sit
in the trees. The light swarmed my face while I recited
sonnets, each last line forlorn but with a tooth in it.
I felt like God, only smaller, flailing my body in and out
of the upper twigs. I lay in a spider's hammock,

the deafening noise of the leaves like Claire's eyelashes.
We were never two sisters sleeping uninterruptedly. Larvae
in their cold dresses. The tree dragged me down against
my will. I ran my hand defiantly through those leafy under-
arms, like a bar of soap in the mouth of a child. A lie

is a cold hand with a light on it. It smacks the cowardly
yellow chrysalis and all the little enemies spill out, all
the little mothers and sisters.

THE OPEN DOOR

They painted the tea roses on their chests with colored pencils.
Tea roses! And so alive! I listened, cried not to live
just in myself. The herons circled close over our roof.
Claire would fan the weight of her hair on Mother's heart,
swinging her long filaments. I waited like a good student

in fencing class. The darkness had a double edge: the light,
a light, that light I'd longed for tipped the shades. They kissed,
they left the clumsy birds behind. With my foil I could have
killed one singing on the balustrade. There was no loneliness
like it: Mother wore a fragrant cashmere jersey; its scent hurt,

dusting me in the corridor. The breath wandered slowly over
their cheeks before reaching me. I imagined buttoning Mother's
clothes until I hid the silly roses, birds behind cages.

SCULPTURE

If there is an end
to the sadness of mothers, sometimes it is in summer:
a few couples pass with their arms around each other.....
Wait! I want to say to them, *stay.* I'd rather have them
a long time tempting me with their shadows
than a daughter stalking the halls
trimming my heart out of our portraits.
The other child, angelic
encumbrance whom I asked to love:
I too had a summer but scorched myself
in front of its paper landscapes. Almost ghosts,
the trees responded, though only a few. I lolled
all day at the window, insubstantially
over her. No one suspected
frustration, my bride,
whittled my sleep with a rasp.

IT WAS LUMINOUS

in the womb. I turned like a mineral with the light
locked inside. Sealed by the mole on my back. When I bathed
with Claire I picked at it—night lily, sister, the water parted
her hair left of center. Left one eye wingless, green. Her
complacency bruised me; a knife trilled in my ear

when she whispered there. Her red disorder of hair—I
imagined we swam in a lake one could slip into, incarnadine,
into some other life. She took her time rinsing, took the time
of someone looking at her, the actress who lays her scarf
on the lake,

stepping deftly across. Mother's black hairs in the tub,
black combs. Could I have floated if I wanted to? The soap
a grenade

SPONGES

The impossibility of my family and the tragedy that keeps me
pursuing it is a moth-eaten story. In a manner of speaking
I was mostly untouched by them, like a concerto for the left
hand, poorly played. Mother occasionally hugged me and imitated

women in the cinema, offering both cheeks to kiss. Claire never
cared, busy uncurling her sleep to drag over Mother's body.
I dreamt too, no differently one imagines, but rose inscrutable.
Today I am studying the Dutch sea captain Vosterloch. He discovered

natives of a bluish color who corresponded by means of sponges
capable of retaining the human voice. To converse from a distance,
they spoke to sponges and sent them to friends who softly
pressed them. The air

is full of alveoli, voices; my pillow an accordion. Perhaps
you have noticed this blue-tone room, conducive to music,
to quiet, to analysis.

SPIRAL IN VERMILION

after Hundertwasser

Sometimes the fog submits to the lake, the lake
to the sky. Na'ria, I loved your sister and I lived
like a yellow sailboat circling
that won't last. Astilbe, paper flower,
                   my foreign girl,
my rendezvous was not with you. Sometimes the innocent
get snagged while floating down a canal
in autumn, concentric, the thousand windows
in red and green, until the gold leaf

itself stops, realizing that hope
is something else. Veiled morning,
contemplative sky. Now, down,
                 why crouch
if not to leap to your wild horse—
auburn, rippling gratefully, relieved
you have arrived.

SAUDADE

THE GLASS HOUSE

I enter at dusk.
The glass shakes in the bedroom.
It was there we all met.

Mother is dead, she is busy.
Father and brother play cards.

Every so often one rises
to clean the bay windows.
The house rests on a body of water.

I enter at dusk.
The glass shakes in the living room.

Mother is eating stale bread.
Father and brother on their knees
eye the precarious water.

The bottom is blue.
The truth is evil and sensual.
Every so often one rises.

Mother is breaking the rock
into sand, the sand into beaches,
the beach into property.

I pick up a rock.
Not that, she says, anything but that.

FRAGMENTS FOR MY VOYEURISTIC BIOGRAPHER

Write that I started in Barcelona
straining against a man on a balcony
Tell how I heard fears on the stair and devoted myself to them

Write those lies because no one is interested in formalities
No one will assume that the stairs were uninhabitable
that the blond man and I were never intimate

Go ahead say I was perverse
letting the others whisper in hotel lobbies
while I went upstairs to finger the spices and ivory

All right I was there I extracted confessions from young women
I stayed in bed all day and listened
knowing I was mistaken I was vulgar

I touched them only at twilight and only because when they left
I was indifferent
I saw their damp eyes their apartments I underwent terrors of lucidity

Imagine their long hairs wiping my back
their nervous kisses

I tell you there was nothing worse than their genuine shudderings
their young lips

Say what you want
I was morbid I was intelligent
I leave you the fragments the furniture the horrible fatigue

EAVESDROPPING AT THE SWIM CLUB, 1934

My parents meet here.
Mother's very tan and clean.
Both look silky and erotic in their suits,
locked arm in arm.
My father still has hair.
Mother is a strong swimmer
with difficulty breathing,
though she fakes it well.
She seems to pull through water with a blade.
It's hard to tell in this heat
who will remember me,
since I don't really belong, like a warning.
I hear him swim around her, squirming.
He mounts a flat-bellied raft
which tremors. There are giggles,
some of them are mine
intruding like a whistle.
They whisper hot kisses.
My father hugs her breasts the way he grabs
two handballs. Sweating, he flexes.
I'm in here purely to hear
him ask her, and mother answer, "I can't."
Bullshit. I listen to her squeal in feigned delight.
It goes through me like a shot.

RED HILLS AND SKY

My grandmother is dirt and I am desert.

Dusk. The datura unnerves me.
I ride out to violate the baked earth.

Hear the gray sage, how its hairs bristle in wind.
I know distance is a woman I must cover at night,
smoothing her clay shawl.

I ride with my angry kiss in my mouth
until I am forced to stop:

red hollyhock against bright blue larkspur,
tell me who has not been quieted by this.

THE MILLER'S DAUGHTER

Nasty King, greedy.·
He crowns you Queen
thinking you can spin
straw into gold.
And then that dirty man
with wheel and magic spindle
who does the work.
I know the situation. The one
who tricked you and the one
who forced. And Daddy
bragging he didn't care
a witch's tit.
Here, you have no name.
I remember that. The twist
is to learn his. Take the King's

fat little wrist in marriage, and hope
the scamp who helped you will forget.
Fat chance. The sneaky wart
comes back to claim the child
unless you guess. You do. He's mad,
and stamps his impish feet and splits in half.
Neat ending. One gets screwed
into the ground (the Devil take him),
and you, for saying Rumpelstilskin,
get to fuck the King. Forever.
I hear him clack the wheel
inside my head
and shove the spindle to and fro
down below. To and fro.

MANY JUNIPERS, HEARTBEATS

The river wasn't cold.
As we swam, I imagined a sonata
with some clouds in the background.

I believed some of it.
To put it into words,
she was the metaphor of a girl.

I would not have known
how to manage my body
if she asked me.

The surface sprawled like a sheet,
and on it I wept for her.
Over the veil which sleeps between women

I wept, and over the sad schoolboy
irrevocably destined for her.
She prayed without opening her lips.

She was cognac, she was frangipani.
They told me finally to stop
my soliciting. How could I have ever

considered her carried away by sentiment—
she wore her inconsolable customs
which chill women and rivers at the source.

I SAW THE SUN RISE IN THE WEST TODAY,

against a bare ailanthus tree in Mexico.
There is this fear I have beginning
with the dawn, where flowers cringe
like survivors at a grave;
a fear of dust, of hooves.

A wind flaps open its miserable God,
the isolated hands with their regrets
slap children. The shadows
pull on the trees,
pull on the laps of the poor,
whose green shawls flutter at the noon sky
turning from pearl to dust.

When evening comes,
it is a dark train of bugs.
I stare at the thick men
going home with a hat over one eye.
I want a man
who remembers little or nothing
of his pure blurred end. The shade
falls like a lover's sad black eyes.
Lie under me, speak of other worlds.

BLUE NUDE

Please take this shy Spanish girl
whom they say you resemble
and ride with her, here are the field poppies
damaged by night, here your blue slumber, your horse.
Take this prayer, which you must surrender
in order to understand, as in moments when you are reduced
to the truth. When you are ready,
the beasts will be there. Let silence go through your heart,
the mild horse your blue one
already stirring toward morning, where it will be white.

SCENE

A shopkeeper ruffles an awning. It is 5 o'clock,
quiet, except where children play

a block away. Poor dogs, they start to want
to die. At the corner a vender

interrupts our embrace
with cries of *knives, knives.* Two strangers,

meeting again after seven years. Is it possible
to be transformed? I speak to silence

my complacency, telling lies that begin
as little hairs and become bestial.

If I lead you down to the lake, isn't the world there
almost unknown? I hold your hand

like a girl who has no intention of stopping
with you. A day-dream,

kites pursue us
with their brilliant tails in a prolonged good-bye.

We find the meaning afterward, somnambulists
on a street where snowflakes fall like white lies,

where shadows spill their stains. We idle
in the street, so soon a photograph.

SEPTEMBER, AT SEA

Ophelia who loved waterlilies. The old man dreaming
in a deck chair. The same boat I took to Tangiers.
It's easy to lean from the boat or order white rum,
as if you still loved me. One stroke of your hair, two.
The bright sun, the sequins of water. I can remember
Italian men sweating in August to fuss over you,
to burn their flecked tongues on your elegant perfume.
Your first gray hairs gathered back like a shawl.
So many nets slung from a boat, so many patterns
of waves. Another cigar-shy young queer ambles by
like a yacht. You simply hated earthquakes, hated
bees. Now I think it's September; yes, I believe
we're at sea.

A DREAM OF BROKEN GLASS

I have a dream of my mother
whose black hair hardens
like the black pebbles of Brazil.

She would make a shell of herself.

I don't trust her, but it doesn't matter.
She is striking glass with a glass.

She is foolish, and has every hope
to appear in this poem as a refined woman.
She would turn, is turning to me now

expecting the cracked glass
to please me. I'm asleep in a woman's body.

She's gone in for the pearl again, the weak
heart I've inherited. I hear pounding,

ten thousand reflections, probably surf.

ONE RADIANT MORNING

Like a smile breaking over teeth,
the teeth of an approaching horse,
one radiant morning
a train from Paraguay arrives.

Girls emerge, a whirling of paper skirts.
Not the sun
but pink itself in their cheeks.
We sit in a cafe across the street.

The clock is not ticking, we think.
We hope they'll enter the park
and lie still in the rosemary.
It's delightful to be shy.

The bells ring, one for each jealous lover.
It's our lives we exaggerate, our misfortune
we watch converge on the square.
One hot day we discover a sombrero full of longing.

A drop could change everything.

SKINNY DAY-MOON AND CRYSTAL

The cabin has two rooms:
upstairs it is summer.
The stove burns
cedar, December. I wait
without a shirt while you sleep.
To quiet my heart I think
of father in Florida;
he forgives my having been
young and wrong about so much.
It snows into the cabin cracks
while you lean your shoulder,
a stranger in my bed
against me. Good-bye father,
flower-laden boat at my feet.
Father, who out here alone
knows what to think? We rock,
charting each other. So long
incandescent men, I've taken my last
look through those portholes, boat
in a bottle floundering
on a swell. Never made me feel
changed. I never could
write the truth because I only
imagined. In this room
perhaps I am lying again,
more likely the body
can no longer contain
its defiance. Even asleep
your throbbing fingers, skull. On earth
there are such places, people are taught
to escape them. I am going to find
my way, my once
unnoticed mouth now with
teethmarks, snowflakes on its lips.
Strange weather, the daylight
of our devouring. Look! from the moon
hangmen are falling and slowly
for our pleasure, like snow.

THE LONG FINGERS OF 1956

Mercy kept me out of the river.
Colder still, the air
burned my young ass.
At night I flew, a cramped
left side, both hands
over my head, the river looked good
down there. A canoe flipped
Abby and me into its empty brace
once, I held on
fingers long gone blue. Grampa died
for nothing one shining afternoon:
no one to start his heart. Pity
and fury aside, who was supposed
to be there wasn't. They told me
September, the last day
in September in the bathroom, home.
Goddamn them. He should be here—
lovers stars the owl spread in the pond—
they're all supposed to be here holding on
the side of moon the living
cling to. What descends effortlessly
through the chestnut leaves? Distant
star, skinny kid seven, grown
homesick in Vermont tonight
hoist two hands overhead for me, for you
not giving in, flying.

SAUDADE

Probably there are other hands waving
in the dream I have of you,
though yours is very white, very frightened,
and certainly other scarves outlined in fog
bow from the deck like grown women,
though yours is the yellow one
shredding into specks.
There is always a white ship with you on it
that leaves from a narrow port,
always my serious hand
fluttering in a meadow at sea level.

I who have followed you only this far
now stop at the dock
and suffer your black, transparent charm.
"Good-bye," a mouth always says, closing its black eye.
And then the left hand, carelessly waving.

A WINTER OF LOVE LETTERS AND A MORNING PRAYER

1.

Snow everywhere,
like your rain. Today I realized I have no illusions
about you beyond the illusion of life itself which I intend
to contrive. Luckily you are haunting and immediate as well.
Of course I'm pursuing this 'unto death' which hasn't

worked before, so help me. Let's not unless for fun, all the time
knowing we devour each other. You know how well I know you. The
quiet. The release. Suddenly wide awake and I mean literally
a billion stars. Most people pass through the applause and through

the applause, forgetting the exquisite moment, the rain, until
there's a foot of snow. Horse at the window, white pine.

2.

I can get away. A simple matter
of being unusually funny at home and then unhinging the latch.
The leaves flying are gay. With you, the bed sash rumples
the light. An aviator in a flight over the Sierras sees erosion

first-hand. You are beautiful, you beguile. You know part of me
disappears at a glance. The light is of no use, gone

like a white mouse. Little night-stones together make a dark
sky. Love me awhile.

3.

                                    The night is quiet.
I wish I lived closer to the sea but beyond that
all is well: the first mild break in winter.

Staring at the stars, the only way I can think of you
is to imagine a migration of birds, washed in the mud
in the morning, their miniscule spring-blue eggs.

As for me, it is difficult to appear mysterious,
what do you think has happened, how unfair!
I acquiesce, but who will I be now apart

from love, I am ashamed of any sign of intelligent
life. The nights mock the mind's momentum, returning
returning. Best to look a little surprised, snatch

from the light its burning and break down the moon
into its white blossoms. Here.

4.

If I could remember you, but I can't. Late light
on the maples, golden birds nesting—those with
a little courage left complete their circles. The witches'
hour: herbs asleep underground, mauve, buff, ochre pockets

where soon we will dip our hands. You are only as distant as
spring, in the slightest movement of the heather as it unwinters.
Dusk motions its sleepy fingers, one, three, five. Where, my love,
are you? an hour closer; in some caress. Between us the silence

is my night-spade. So much has fallen, the days themselves, the dry
leaves of beeches supposed to keep all winter.

5.

In this chapel those who kneel are bigger than those
standing, and those who bow down stand gigantic. You
delve deeper into the dark at first and panic, but you
need to *know* all the same. Otherwise how many years pass

like hummingbirds forced to fly at glass? The ivy
fields, red, gray, and the brides in them want only to sway,
to serve the music from the chapel, the chapel far now
from the sea. No greater than a shell,

the soul is distant and within reach. From the opening
strings the white meadowsweet, eyes who never close.

6.

after Emil Nolde

My first flower grew
from grandmother's red hair, the sweet and cool
of the evening. Then the special snow-covered flower,
whose large white shoulders held up the sky.

(If you would touch me, once, on the eyes, once
on the lips.) In summer the red and yellow cliffs left
giant teethmarks on their undersides *(on the neck, on the back*
of the neck.) The high moon in half, Florence in her pink

dress against the pale-green sky, my darling how long
since you cried over something? *(for joy, if you would, with*
your hand.) The walls of my childhood are glass and through one
I see the red poppy where there is a long line of trees:

I sit on the floor, I sit on a chair, I move the chair closer.
It is still there.

7.

The beeches are vibrant because there is black
in them against the horizon. Hundreds of calla lilies,
the sun's fingers nudge the wide-hipped clouds. Here we are

summoned into the world: I pass those whom I pleased
out of disdain to create, what, a style? And those
sulking, coaxed by the beech in full bloom. The bark

was written on, names I can't remember. How long
is you hair now, how long will it be? Hang discretion
and its three-cornered nuts! I love you and vow

I'm no longer idle, climbing a long line of beeches
like lace. Jane with sunspots; with, almost, grace.

8.

A poet begins a song and something in the country
completes it, asking, 'Weren't you happy as a girl?'
or saying, 'Blue eyes and white curly hair, a pleasure.'
Tension, like how children dress brightly

and are dirty. In the forest new snow, gorgeous
enough to excuse all those moonless nights. Not
to be mistaken for anyone else, your arrival advances
with its perfect sway like spring rain nervously

and passionately summoned. One loses oneself, caught in mid-
gesture, a bear in the wood, seen? Otherwise months go by,
no desire to see anyone. I miss the most innocent harmonies.
It is easier not to write. The bear, was it there, leaves

shadows stirring their padded feet. Approaching with care
you flash your white teeth.

9.

If I have to wait on this threshold
I will never know the trail to the sea.
Remember the afternoons you brought the dunes to me

like shuddering bodies, the sudden sandy stares.
When do you return, which way
and what music while I wait?

Maybe this is almost beautiful
alone—vague nocturne behind me,
late, and the night-sails flecked with crows.

Turning, I see you
as though through water and never
quite this way again: your scarf moves,

a gull rising on a string, and slowly the string
catches wind to sea.

MAY YOU ALWAYS BE THE DARLING OF FORTUNE

March 10th and the snow flees like eloping brides
into rain. The imperceptible change begins
out of an old rage and glistens, chaste, with its new
craving, spring. May your desire always overcome

your need; your story that you have to tell,
enchanting, mutable, may it fill the world
you believe: a sunny view, flowers lunging
from the sill, the quilt, the chair, all things

fill with you and empty and fill. And hurry because
now as I tire of my studied abandon, counting
the days, I'm sad. Yet I trust your absence, in everything
wholly evident: the rain in the white basin and I

vigilant.

AUTUMN, EXPLODED VIEW

SELF-CONTAINED VIEW: I AM A WOMAN

I said. I was drunk. I sat in t-shirt and shorts and basked
in the illusion of time to myself. I had a great figure
in clothes where my small scars were hinted at. People watched
like they observe themselves sometimes, say, peeling an orange,
o isn't this sensual they think in an adult circumspect way.
Lips are popular. We groan into their part, that russet
brown, oh oh that russet that, ah. Once in South America
someone screamed eat me in a respectable hotel lobby. Oh those
Spanish boys knew what she meant. In the elevator. I have to

prolong this because women like it that way. Only three men
have ever spoken to me about failure. Inside my hazel eyes,
blue and green flares shoot off, impossible to detect unless
you love me. And didn't everyone then: drinking warm Bordeaux,
I held their hands. So many insisted on being included so
who was I to renounce them. We make ourselves sick. I was
drunk when I arrived and am cold now. So little of me is
destructive. We make ourselves live.

CHARRED VIEW: NIGHT FIRES

Night after night, from curtain to ghost to cloven reflection,
I sit at my desk. At daybreak I think, *someone's been here,* blowing
the coals, kissing my cool head. There's more than that—the beginning
is lonely. But who can't love the heart of the galaxy, earth
circling, making its turns in the void, two children spinning
a top, who can't be distracted. All bone and eye at this hour, I
glimpse Venus, her, or something of her, but only her in the iris
of the sky. All else rage burnt out or burning inward, darkness

of pupil, of presentiment. Aren't I wooing the sunrise, musn't I
bow down and dig for it, exposing the slightest red here, the
blackest pink there until, kicking the char off the very sun, dawn?
Such a soundless quake. The way it hurts to wake because uncon-
sciously I destroy what I write. This intrigue will continue; I can't
help the child who has lost his toy, the girl whose mother
is dead. They, who knew nothing of today, rise after the raven
sun, black where it bruised last night.

IMMACULATE VIEW

love: the power of lust turned generous, the power of sleep
to enter dream: who has not wanted to climb on a warm
day up again toward those sunny hills: remember, how
the whispers sweep us like grass fires: there's always memory
telling our fortune, with a purpose beyond the telling: to pearl
the grainy black day with color where all things long to persist
in their being, as in the beginning: violet cumuli gilded
with lightning, creating space for us as we advance: to think
something never before possible, pristine stone, menhirs,
telluric shocks, daylight earth: o visibility, white as warm
quartz: I sleep and sleep and my father rows out at night,
who taught me, not in pleasure alone but with a kind of fear
to touch another's body: tangible and liquescent, true, un-
tying the scarf from my eyes: what it's like in the void, fierce,
defiant, sad saraband: not with fear alone but in a blind
of pleasure to touch a prescient body:

DISTANT FIGURE IN BLACK MERINO

Gray sky, gray smoke, your white face fair, far. Fields
fallen into desuetude. Barely lit shadowy sides of stems
a warm black-green; streak of red on the horizon. I wear
a Jewish star against its rough edge; walking, I suck on it.
I am always young knowing you are out here, though far, lovely
among late clover. Nearsighted, I love the bare morning and black
night. Afternoons, with their orange slices, their apples
and cream, pass into other hands. I have learned to trace

your outline as quickly as lightning. With or without moon,
your white bones strain shining nightly against the dark. To
infuriate dawn, the shock of your coat in the haze. Although
it isn't right to count on it, your repose stands out, serious,
mysterious: tirelessly in the background my dark cypress or light
star. Your distant syncopation, unseen, soothes me. All nerve
and grasp, what do I, what do the woods describe; what do
the woods desire? Their membraned limbs untether last leaves.
Soon we will be alone, one body.

NOT EVER

*So hot so early. Gold light thrown onto the water to feed
little animals on their backs*—a dream I wake from to a warm
autumn day. Dandelion puffs and flies crowd the air. Horsehair
and apple-smell. There's an ache in my back and neck and still
three cords to stack. Rust-coppery leaves crack their spines.
Stark blue days, reminiscent of Greek dawns: harbor light, the un-
divided waters—think of it! the variable waves. Fantasies
lace low-tide where pairs of lovers bury the past in blond
sand. Because if the universe contracts, it hasn't enough mass

to begin again. The million suns painting Spruce Mountain
circle and hold at my window. They break the rules, they enter
the room, gold-leafing my oak floor. The other day I decided not
to have children. Not now. . . . *To shut out the light or let it in
as I please.* But I miss their talk, a language I hear as a breeze
to ruffle me. The sun easily hides behind a cloud. Little animals
on their backs hate the coming of winter. They scamper suddenly,
those that can get to their feet.

THE HEART CLIMBS DEVILISHLY BACK INTO THE BODY; OR, FIELD OF RED THISTLES

Noon, noon, noon, the muted creek, the mare locked in the barn.
Winter to break, about to break, about to mother-me-down. I dream
of her in a clear, plastic suit cracked down the back and tearing,
which I have to stop. Finding myself sobbing periodically, mother
of hard vinyl like a telephone with her flesh exposed keeps asking in
the high voice of the mortally wronged, what does anyone know about
poetry, or care? Who looks through Beaudelaire's windows, who sees him
undressing there? In time we discover the hard blue sky is hard.
And the summer figs, the cherished tan of last season? now only glare

at me, and the leaves by the road-side pith and collect. I trembled
when I heard their words and the empty minds of the poor scavenged
trees. Moon moon moon in them, owl, hawk, owl. All saying now
Halloween, now, blaspheme of roses, cancelled weddings, interior
monologues. Inside the barn the whiskers on the horse gather
frost. And the steam knocks, and the wicks sputter. Magnificent
sunset, mother going down. Inside the house her heart climbs back
into her body, bloodying the back steps. The action begins again,
the failing light, the underside of the moon imagining me here.
Dusk pulls a mauve tarp across a field of red thistles, and catches.

BENEATH THE HOARFROST IT IS SUMMER IN VIENNA

Don't take my word for it: the change I'm talking about doesn't occur
by degrees, it happens suddenly: under the hoarfrost something huge
and multiplicious throbs, dazzling as the Alps. My body shifts
under three layers of sweaters; I'm in some mood whose peaks are
covered with fresh snow, cool and distant. A few hints come at once
that we are lovers: the hard ground palpitates, as if invaded by
periwinkles in ice. Birch bark peels back, revealing the fine particles
of a life to which I must give way, stripped pink and settling
in for winter. The clouds are better off by themselves, waiting like
memories to turn me inside. The chaste spirit of winter nights, animal-

safe like a secret self, rumbles the chambers where we surrender. I
throw a beautiful checkered wool blanket over our shoulders. It's not
our love I fear, but that my cold sporting life will be arrested
in summer in mid-air, forever blue skies and rice. We wash our hair
in ice water, but all the time sweat runs off you threateningly
friendly. Clusters of smoke escape the stove-pipe like summer grapes;
the frail white body of the past loses shape in the sky. Spirit of
lonely Sundays, burst of insouciance quelled like a sunset every time
I admit I need you. I need you. The powder is still warm where you
whisper *lie down.*

YOUNG GIRLS IN HATS SMOKING CIGARETTES

The eucalyptuses droop. They still have to recover from the fires
of '71. On top of that, a few froze in the hills that same year.
The royal bluejays on the east coast now are reminiscent of those
predatory days in California, kissed on one side and rebuked by
afternoon. Here, roads are made slippery by sleighs. Young girls
squeal; their hearts stop, red mouths garnering their next whoop.
They eat the snow, they devour the scene, becoming older, becoming
what they'll remember: someone chopping wood, someone along a road
taking notes, destined to undress the prettiest. A glint of summer
in him, red-cheeked, sweat at the hairline. What of the eucalyptus

leaves, and of the irises that caught fire under those leaves, under
the dark-blue cloud of those years, what of the cloud, blackened into
a recurring dream: how young girls bolt from indoors, bloom, light
cigarettes and, in disdain, remember too well how men fail: no one sees
the white husky in the snow until he pisses. Their lipstick is on
fire, their lips peel from my own. I watch this fire and regret-
ably, I snuff it out. It is 9:30 p.m. in Montreal. I'm with my
mistress. We're at the window where a whiff of California, red and
orange hats go bobbing by, heartbeats of rue, too quickly, too true.

6 A.M.

I want to be bad, but I'm not. There's a warm breath
off the bridle path. The last groans of sex recede, light
musk on a woman's wrist. A sudden clearing. Birds, almost,
where I'm out walking. This season's animals? We're beginners
making tracks: I'm proving how at last you meet and turn
him away. The wilderness you walk out of is thawing, different
by day, by night: that incredible story of the man you waited for.
Cats stir sleepers at this hour. Your son gets up to pee.
My body retraces the last time, tenderly, it had no desire

to be understood, like a nose-bleed. The sexually responsive
ground-swell is a form in which we see our excess, cryptically.
Tobogganers will slide right by here later, hair held by cold
barrettes, the intimacy of hearts and hard ground. Not for you
alone the clock-radio prepares *when I look into your blue skies, baby....–*
I'm also in a dream, exaggerating early morning moans, the way
earth hardens, opens, runs. Skunk spray's next; snowstorms
demystified to rain. Drift, love; the hands haven't yet signaled
with their bloody tips.

5 A.M.

Spicier. The best thing would be snow, and soon.
Twice the water has frozen because there's no
ground cover. I wake to let the tap drip, get cold
cider and decide to dress. I'll have to bank the
pipes with styrofoam and straw. Released, it's un-
expectedly warm. Ice thins to isinglass. I pace,
I take our last taut gratuitous embrace and fling
myself into the slush. Guilty over two lovers in one
week, I dirty the gravel with abandon. Then a crow's
humiliating *flock, flock.*
                            Smoke backing up
and belching. I watch the house. Night nightens
on its way to the shortest day of the year.
The door is gusted shut and my eyes dark, my brief
body that contains the future. How long am I
willing to wait? I see now the months and years,
interiors in blue, in pale, in bed. Is it to end
nobly that we lie down for so long dying
to be touched there, and there? How well I look, and you
and you and you. Foul, I help myself to friends.

CASIDA OF THE LIGHT FANTASTIC

after Lorca

The sloe-eyed houri
peering out above her veil
sees it, and cannot help smiling.
The light permits certain cruelties.
To those who know how to receive
the light is on them, on their lower lip,
and always on the verge of falling:

it falls into the valley below the veil
as it falls into a hall overheated in summer.
The light is not chance.
The light is sorry to close the door
on the angels, ill-timed, in heavy overcoats;
to see desire, older now,
without the ruby in her belly.

The light sees everything
 that very likely is living
through the happiest days of its life.
The light will always come back
as and when it can. You remember,
and then you see the white petals
move uninterruptedly, but falling away,
light-years strung like ornaments,
that never break by themselves.

So many dead before me,
moths circling their hearts.
 Their hearts cast out
armies of filaments
to catch the light.

NOTES

RED HILLS AND SKY: title from a painting by Georgia O'Keeffe.

SAUDADE: longing, nostalgia, daydreaming, remembrance, home-sickness, deep, bittersweet desire to live a moment again (Portuguese).

SPONGES: the description of Vosterloch is adapted from a passage in the *Couirrier Veritable,* 1632, as noted by Jean Cocteau in *Opium.*

Jane Miller was born April 27, 1949, in New York and raised in New Jersey. She earned degrees from Penn State, California State University at Humboldt, and The University of Iowa. In 1978, she won the YM-WHA/The Nation's Discovery Award. She lives in Plainfield, Vermont, and teaches at Goddard College.